American Biographies

MALCOLM X

Gail Fay

Chicago, Illinois

www.capstonepub.com
Visit our website to find out more information about Heinemann-Raintree books.

To order:
☎ Phone 800-747-4992
🖥 Visit www.capstonepub.com
to browse our catalog and order online.

Edited by Abby Colich, Megan Cotugno, and Laura Hensley
Designed by Philippa Jenkins
Original illustrations © Capstone Global Library Limited 2011
Illustrated by Oxford Designers and Illustrators
Picture research by Tracy Cummins
Originated by Capstone Global Library Limited
Printed and bound in China by Leo Paper Group

16 15 14 13 12
10 9 8 7 6 5 4 3 2 1

Library of Congress Cataloging-in-Publication Data
Fay, Gail.
  Malcolm X / Gail Fay.
    p. cm.—(American biographies)
  Includes bibliographical references and index.
  ISBN 978-1-4329-6456-6 (hb)—ISBN 978-1-4329-6467-2 (pb) 1. X, Malcolm, 1925-1965—Juvenile literature. 2. Black Muslims—Biography—Juvenile literature. 3. African Americans—Biography—Juvenile literature. I. Title.
  BP223.Z8L573365 2013
  320.54'6092—dc23   2011037581
  [B]

Acknowledgments
The author and publishers are grateful to the following for permission to reproduce copyright material: AP Photo: pp. 7 (Henry Griffin), 14 (Angela Rowlings), 17, 31, 33, 36 (WCBS-TV News), 37, 39 (Charles Rex Arbogast), 40 (Chad Rachman), 41 (Patrick J. Cunningham); Corbis: pp. 5 (© Bettmann), 10 (© Bettmann), 20 (© CORBIS), 25 (© Bettmann), 26 (© Bettmann), 29 (© Flip Schulke), 38 (© Flip Schulke); Getty Images: pp. 15 (Time Life Pictures/Timepix), 19 (Richard Saunders/Pictorial Parade/Hulton Archive), 22 (Michael Ochs Archive), 23 (Richard Saunders/Pictorial Parade/Archive Photos), 35 (Robert L. Haggins/Time Life Pictures); Library of Congress Prints & Photographs Division: pp. 4, 6, 9, 11; Rex USA: p. 12 (Everett Collection); The Art Archive: p. 8 (Global Book Publishing).

Cover photograph of Malcolm X reproduced with permission from Newscom (KRT).

Every effort has been made to contact copyright holders of material reproduced in this book. Any omissions will be rectified in subsequent printings if notice is given to the publisher.

Contents

Some words are shown in bold, **like this**.
These words are explained in the glossary.

"The Angriest Black Man in America"

Malcolm X described himself as "the angriest black man in America." What was he so angry about?

Malcolm X once said, "If you don't stand for something, you will fall for anything." The thing Malcolm stood for was freedom for black people.

Black people were sometimes called "colored." Because of Jim Crow laws, signs such as this were posted near drinking fountains, hotels, restaurants, waiting rooms, and other public places.

Segregation and discrimination

Malcolm X hated the way white people treated black people in the United States. **Slavery** had been outlawed in 1865, but white people still acted like they were better than black people. These white people created **Jim Crow laws** to keep the **races** separate. According to these laws, black people could not go to the same schools, use the same public restrooms, or live in the same neighborhoods as white people. This separation of races is called **segregation**.

Malcolm was angry about the **discrimination** that resulted from segregation. Since white people made the Jim Crow laws, they controlled where black people lived and worked. Black neighborhoods were more run-down than white neighborhoods. Black people had lower-paying jobs than white people. Jim Crow laws prevented black people from going to college and from getting high-paying jobs.

Malcolm was angry because black people felt stuck. They had to go along with segregation because there were consequences if they did not. They might be threatened or beaten by **white supremacists**. White supremacists believe whites are better than nonwhites. Some white supremacists **lynched**, or killed, black people who broke the rules of segregation.

5

The March on Washington was a key event in the civil rights movement. More than 200,000 black and white people protested the discrimination against blacks.

The civil rights movement

Malcolm X was so angry that he took action. He became an important leader during the **civil rights movement** of the 1950s and 1960s. The civil rights movement was an organized protest against segregation and discrimination against black people. It started in Alabama and spread to other states.

Another important leader in the civil rights movement was Martin Luther King, Jr. Like Malcolm X, King wanted to stop segregation. He wanted better living conditions and job opportunities for blacks. Both men were powerful and convincing speakers. Both men made enemies because of what they said. But these two leaders were also very different in their beliefs. Look at the chart for a summary of these differences.

	Malcolm X	Martin Luther King, Jr.
Message	Blacks are better than whites	Blacks and whites are equal
Goals	Equal rights for black people Separation of blacks and whites	Equal rights for black people **Integration** of blacks and whites
Methods	"Any means necessary" If whites use violence, blacks can use violence in return	Nonviolent protests "Turn the other cheek"— do not fight violence with violence

Martin Luther King, Jr., (left) and Malcolm X met only once, and it was by accident. They both happened to be in Washington, D.C., on March 26, 1964.

Martin Luther King, Jr.

(1929–1968)

Martin Luther King, Jr., was born in Atlanta, Georgia. King was a good student. He skipped two grades and went to an all-black college at age 15. Later, King became a Baptist preacher, like his father and grandfather. King is best known for his peaceful protests during the civil rights movement. On April 4, 1968, King was **assassinated** by a man named James Earl Ray.

Troubled Childhood

Malcolm X's birth name was Malcolm Little. His mother, Louise, had light-brown skin because her father was white. Malcolm had light skin and reddish-brown hair, like his mother.

Malcolm X was born on May 19, 1925, in Omaha, Nebraska.

Like father, like son

Malcolm's father, Earl, was a Baptist preacher. He was also a black **activist** in the Universal Negro Improvement Association, or UNIA. As a black activist, Earl tried to improve the lives of black people. The UNIA was founded by another black activist named Marcus Garvey (see the box).

Garvey started the UNIA to spread his ideas about **black nationalism**. Black nationalists believe black Americans should live separately from whites. They believe blacks should have their own businesses, leaders, and schools. Garvey said black people should leave the United States and go back to Africa to form their own nation.

White supremacists threatened to hurt Earl Little and his family because of his teachings on black nationalism. Reverend Little moved his family to Milwaukee, Wisconsin, and then to Lansing, Michigan (see map on page 13). But the threats did not stop.

Marcus Garvey

(1887–1940)

Marcus Garvey was born in Jamaica. He moved to England in 1912 and met blacks who wanted to form their own nation, separate from the British Empire. In 1916 Garvey moved once again, this time to the United States. He started teaching black nationalism. Garvey raised money to buy ships to take blacks back to Africa. In 1925 he went to jail for raising money illegally. Around 1927 the U.S. government sent Garvey back to Jamaica.

Garvey published several books and newspapers containing his ideas on black nationalism.

The Ku Klux Klan (KKK) is a white supremacist group that wears white robes and terrorizes black people. Malcolm's family was threatened by the Black Legion, a group that broke off from the KKK.

Father dies

In Lansing, Michigan, Reverend Little led the local UNIA meetings. Sometimes Malcolm went to meetings with his father. At a young age, Malcolm heard how black people needed to stand up for themselves.

When Malcolm was four, a white supremacist group known as the Black Legion burned down his family's house. The Littles barely escaped alive. Then, two years later, Reverend Little was run over by a streetcar. Louise believed the Black Legion killed her husband and placed his body on the tracks to make it look like an accident.

Mother has a breakdown

After her husband's death, Louise struggled to care for her children. The few jobs she found did not pay well. Sometimes Louise made only 50 cents a day. She had to get help from the state **welfare** office. This office provides food and other necessities to people who are very poor. Malcolm's family was one of the poorest in Lansing. Malcolm had to wear his brothers' old clothes. He often went to school hungry. Malcolm started stealing food from the store.

In 1939 Malcolm's mother had an emotional breakdown. She could not handle the pressure of caring for the family alone. She was sent to a mental hospital. Malcolm and his siblings went to live in different homes.

This photo shows Lansing, Michigan, about the time Malcolm lived there.

A new start

After Malcolm's mother went into the hospital, Malcolm moved to a group home in Mason, Michigan. It was a place for neglected, or unwanted, children. Malcolm was 14 when he moved.

At the group home, Malcolm had his own bedroom for the first time.

A couple named the Swerlins directed the group home. They liked Malcolm, and Malcolm liked them. He worked hard to please the Swerlins. Malcolm's behavior improved. He stopped stealing and started studying. During the second semester, Malcolm was elected seventh-grade president.

Turning point

One day Malcolm's English teacher, Mr. Ostrowski, asked what career Malcolm wanted as an adult. Malcolm said he wanted to be a lawyer. The teacher told Malcolm that was not a realistic goal for a black person. At that time most law schools did not accept black students. Mr. Ostrowski suggested Malcolm choose something more practical, such as being a carpenter.

Malcolm was hurt. He had better grades than most of his white classmates, and they wanted to be doctors and police officers. But because Malcolm was black, his hard work and good grades did not matter. Malcolm quit school. He wondered what the point was if it did not help him get a good job. In 1941 he moved to Boston, Massachusetts (see the map), to live with his half sister.

This map highlights the different U.S. cities Malcolm lived in throughout his life.

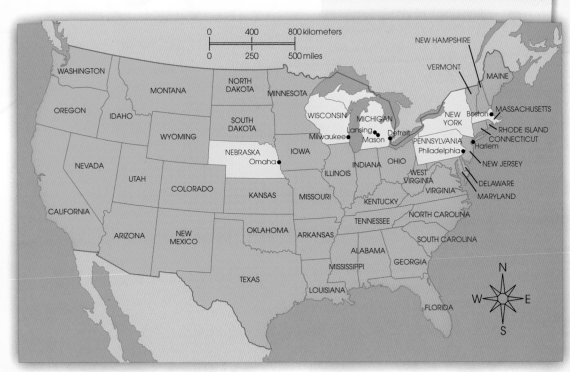

From Criminal to Convert

Malcolm's half sister, Ella, lived in the Roxbury neighborhood of Boston, Massachusetts. There was a large black population there.

Ella owned this house in Roxbury. Malcolm considered Ella to be the most confident black woman he ever met.

Did you know?

Around 1943, Malcolm started going by the nickname "Detroit Red." Malcolm had reddish-brown hair, and he had lived in Lansing and Mason, Michigan, near Detroit.

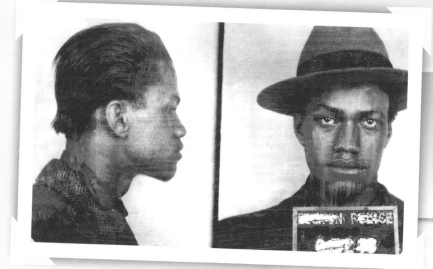

Malcolm was 20 years old when he was arrested for robbery.

Exciting new life

Fifteen-year-old Malcolm liked the busy streets, loud music, and pool halls in one section of Roxbury. Here, black people had their own way of dressing. They wore fancy **zoot suits** and wide-brimmed hats. They "conked," or straightened, their curly hair. (Malcolm's hair is conked in the picture above.) They also had their own way of walking and talking that set them apart from white people.

Malcolm met a man named Shorty at one of the Roxbury pool halls. He got Malcolm a job shining shoes at the Roseland State Ballroom. Shorty also taught Malcolm how he should act, so that white customers would give him large tips.

Detroit Red gets caught

Malcolm later got a job on the railroad. He started as a dishwasher and later sold sandwiches. Working on the train allowed Malcolm to travel. In 1943 he went to Harlem, a neighborhood in New York City, and he decided to stay. In Harlem, Malcolm began making money illegally. He got into trouble with a gang and had to move back to Boston.

In Boston, Malcolm started stealing again. He was part of a group that robbed houses. In January 1946 Malcolm got caught. He was arrested and sentenced to 10 years in jail.

Prison life

In February 1946 Malcolm entered prison. The building had no running water or flushing toilets. His cell was barely long enough to allow Malcolm to lie down.

While in prison, Malcolm decided to educate himself. He read a lot of books, and he studied the dictionary to improve his vocabulary.

Introduction to the Nation of Islam

Malcolm's family wrote letters and visited him in jail. Malcolm's brother Reginald told Malcolm about his new religion, the **Nation of Islam**. Only black people could join this religion. Members were called **Black Muslims**. They worshiped a God called Allah, who spoke to his people through a black man named Elijah Muhammad (see the box). Members called Muhammad "the Messenger."

Reginald told Malcolm that white people were evil. They wanted to rule over blacks. Malcolm remembered what he had read in the history books. White people brought Africans to the Americas to be their **slaves**.

Fact VS. Fiction

The Nation of Islam is not the same as traditional **Islam**. Traditional **Muslims** do not believe Elijah Muhammad was Allah's messenger.

Elijah Muhammad

(1897–1975)

Elijah Poole was born in Georgia. His parents had been slaves. Poole joined the Nation of Islam when it first started in 1930. He later changed his name to Elijah Muhammad. In 1934 Muhammad became the leader, and he remained the Messenger of Allah until his death.

Elijah Muhammad led the Nation of Islam for 41 years.

Reginald also said blacks should live separately from whites. Black people needed their own leaders and businesses. Malcolm's father used to say the same thing. The more Malcolm thought about Reginald's religion and beliefs, the more they made sense to him.

Conversion

Malcolm wrote to Elijah Muhammad, and the leader wrote back. Elijah Muhammad did not blame Malcolm for stealing. He said white people had forced him to steal because they prevented him from getting a job that made enough money.

Shortly after receiving this letter, Malcolm **converted** to the Nation of Islam. His behavior immediately changed. He stopped gambling. Black Muslims were taught to keep their bodies pure, so Malcolm stopped smoking. He cut his hair short like other Black Muslim men. Malcolm also told many black prisoners about Allah and the Nation of Islam.

A new name

In August 1952, Malcolm was released from prison, nearly four years early. He was 27 years old. Malcolm moved to Detroit, Michigan (see the map on page 13), and lived with his brother Wilfred. Malcolm started attending Temple Number One in Detroit. It was called Temple Number One because it was the first temple founded by Elijah Muhammad.

In late 1952, Malcolm met Elijah Muhammad for the first time. He convinced Malcolm to stop using his last name. According to Muhammad, "Little" was the name given to Malcolm's family when they were slaves. Black Muslims used the letter "X" instead of their slave name. It represented their lost African name. From then on, Malcolm Little was known as Malcolm X.

Did you know?

After he became a Black Muslim, Malcolm spent more time in the sun to darken his light skin.

At a Nation of Islam meeting, women wear all white and sit separately from the men. Here, Malcolm (center with glasses) prepares to speak in Washington, D.C.

Minister

Malcolm was disappointed that there were so many empty seats at the meetings in Temple Number One. Detroit had many black people who needed to hear the messages taught there. They needed to hear how they could help themselves. Malcolm started visiting black neighborhoods to tell them about the **Nation of Islam**. His goal was to bring as many black people as possible to the temple.

Malcolm X delivered many intense sermons as a Nation of Islam minister.

A powerful preacher

Malcolm soon earned a leadership role. In the summer of 1953, he became the assistant minister of Temple Number One. In the beginning of 1954, Elijah Muhammad sent Malcolm to Boston to establish a new temple. When that temple was running smoothly, Malcolm was sent to Philadelphia, Pennsylvania (see the map on page 13). In each place, his powerful preaching attracted many new believers. Malcolm told black people to stop waiting for the "white devils" to give them equal rights. Blacks needed to clean up their lives and take action.

Not all blacks agreed with Malcolm's message. Some thought he was making things worse for black people by making whites angry. But Malcolm did not change his words.

In June 1954 Elijah Muhammad made Malcolm minister of Temple Number Seven in Harlem (see the map on page 13). Number Seven was the second most important temple in the Nation of Islam. This was a big step for Malcolm.

Did you know?

Between 1952 and 1963, membership in the Nation of Islam increased from 500 to 30,000 people. Malcolm's convincing preaching probably contributed to this increase.

Betty was a nursing student when she and Malcolm met.

Betty X

In 1956 a woman named Betty Sanders visited the Harlem temple. A friend had invited her to hear Malcolm speak. Betty liked Malcolm's message and continued going to meetings. At the end of 1958, Betty joined the Nation of Islam and became Betty X. In January 1958, Malcolm and Betty got married.

Did you know?

Not everyone in the Nation of Islam received an "X" as their last name. It was only given to people who applied for membership and were dedicated followers.

A hero in Harlem

In April 1957, Harlem police officers attacked an unarmed black man named Johnson Hinton. Hinton was then dragged to the police station.

After Malcolm found out, he and 50 **Black Muslims** marched to the police station. The men stood at attention like an army while Malcolm went inside. He demanded to see Hinton. Meanwhile, hundreds of blacks from the neighborhood joined the Black Muslims.

Hinton was badly beaten. Malcolm demanded that Hinton be taken to the hospital. The crowd followed the ambulance on foot. After making sure Hinton was receiving medical care, Malcolm dismissed the crowd.

Malcolm X became a hero in Harlem. He had stood up to the white police officers. Afterward, many blacks in Harlem became interested in the Nation of Islam. Membership in Temple Number Seven greatly increased.

Malcolm conducts a sermon at Temple Number Seven in Harlem in 1963.

New responsibilities

Later in 1957, Elijah Muhammad made Malcolm the national spokesperson for the Nation of Islam. Malcolm traveled to cities nationwide. He preached to large crowds of black people and helped start new temples. Malcolm shared the teachings of Elijah Muhammad in several black newspapers. Within a couple of years, many blacks across the United States knew about Malcolm X.

New publicity

In 1959 white Americans were introduced to Malcolm X through a television show about the Nation of Islam. The **documentary** film was called *The Hate That Hate Produced*. It was the first time white people had really heard the message of Elijah Muhammad and his followers. The documentary showed clips of Malcolm and other ministers preaching that blacks needed to separate from whites. It showed Black Muslim children being taught that whites are "devils." It also showed the Fruit of Islam, which was an army of young men within the Nation of Islam who were trained to fight.

Fact VS. Fiction

Traditional **Islam** does not teach that white people are devils.

The documentary explained Muhammad's teaching that blacks should avoid using white-owned businesses whenever possible. Black people should shop at black-owned business such as this one.

White viewers were shocked and afraid. They already knew that black people wanted equal rights and better opportunities. Some white people became **activists** and joined the peaceful protests of the **civil rights movement**. But this was the first time white people realized that some black people saw them as evil.

Many black people were also upset by the film. They thought the Black Muslims were encouraging violence. Martin Luther King, Jr., and other black activists thought it was better to protest peacefully.

Malcolm became especially popular with young black men who were angry about **discrimination**. They liked Malcolm's message about fighting for equal rights.

Malcolm becomes a superstar

After the film came out, people wanted to know more about the Nation of Islam. People wondered whether Black Muslims really taught that whites are evil. They wondered if Black Muslims really wanted a separate nation. Reporters started interviewing Malcolm for answers. Malcolm soon became a celebrity.

Malcolm also became more **militant**, or aggressive. In the early 1960s, violence against black people increased. In one case, four black girls were killed when **white supremacists** bombed the Sixteenth Street Baptist Church in Birmingham, Alabama. Malcolm pointed out that peaceful **sit-ins** were not working. Black people needed to fight back.

Malcolm and the FBI

During this same time, Malcolm also attracted the attention of the Federal Bureau of Investigation (FBI). The FBI thought Malcolm might be planning a black **revolution**, or rebellion. They wondered if the Nation of Islam was training young men to take over the United States government.

Around 1960 the FBI started spying on Malcolm. They paid black people to join the Nation of Islam. These people would report on what Malcolm was doing and saying. This spying continued for about four years.

Fact VS. Fiction

Some people thought Malcolm X was a communist. Communists believe all people should be in the same social class. They believe the lower classes should revolt, or fight back, if necessary. Though some of his ideas were similar, Malcolm X was not a communist. He said he could never be a communist, since communists do not believe in God.

True Muslim

As Malcolm became more popular, some people within the **Nation of Islam** became jealous. They started spreading lies about Malcolm. They told Elijah Muhammad that Malcolm was trying to take over the Nation of Islam.

At the same time, Malcolm and Muhammad had some disagreements. Muhammad thought Malcolm was too outspoken about using violence if necessary. Malcolm thought **Black Muslims** should work with black people of all religions, but Muhammad disagreed. Then Malcolm discovered that Muhammad had broken some rules that all Black Muslims were supposed to obey. Malcolm felt betrayed. Muhammad had created these important rules. How could he break them?

Fact VS. Fiction

Some reporters made it sound like Malcolm X was happy that President Kennedy had been **assassinated**. That is not true. Malcolm said the president's death was an example of "chickens coming home to roost." What he meant was that the United States had accepted violence against black people, and now violence had taken the president's life.

Martin Luther King, Jr., (second from left) and others met with President Kennedy (fourth from right) to discuss the March on Washington. Malcolm did not participate. He wondered why blacks would protest with the "white devils" they were protesting against.

Malcolm is silenced

On November 22, 1963, President John F. Kennedy was assassinated by Lee Harvey Oswald. About two weeks later, Malcolm spoke at a Black Muslim rally. Afterward reporters asked Malcolm what he thought about Kennedy's assassination. Elijah Muhammad had told all ministers to be quiet about the president's death, but Malcolm still commented (see the box). As a result, Elijah Muhammad silenced Malcolm. He was not allowed to speak in public for 90 days.

Malcolm leaves the Nation of Islam

Malcolm was hurt by Elijah Muhammad's decision to prevent him from speaking publicly. He also thought Muhammad had another reason for silencing him. Maybe he believed the lies about Malcolm wanting to take over. Maybe he wanted to silence Malcolm forever. Malcolm had heard rumors that someone in the Nation of Islam wanted him dead.

In March 1964, Malcolm announced that he was leaving the Nation of Islam. He started a new organization called Muslim Mosque, Inc. His goal was the same. Malcolm wanted the freedom of 22 million black Americans "by any means necessary."

Malcolm knew this was a dangerous decision. He had already made enemies because of his words against white people. Now many Black Muslims thought he was a **traitor**. Several members warned Malcolm that his decision would have serious consequences.

Fact VS. Fiction

Traditional **Islam** does not teach that blacks are better than whites. It teaches that all **races** are equal.

Muhammad Ali

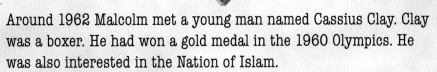

(born 1942)

Around 1962 Malcolm met a young man named Cassius Clay. Clay was a boxer. He had won a gold medal in the 1960 Olympics. He was also interested in the Nation of Islam.

In 1964 Clay fought the defending heavyweight champion, Sonny Liston. Clay won after six rounds. Shortly after the fight, Clay announced that he was a member of the Nation of Islam. He also said he had a new name—Muhammad Ali. Ali became one of the greatest heavyweight boxers of all time.

Muhammad Ali (left) is famous for saying he could "float like a butterfly, sting like a bee" in the boxing ring.

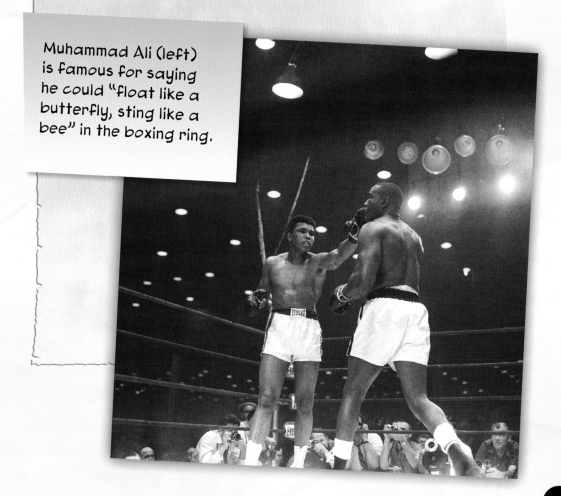

Traditional Islam

Islam is one of the largest religions in the world. About 23 percent of all the people in the world are **Muslims**. Islam teaches five basic principles:

1. Worship Allah and no one else.
2. Pray five times a day.
3. Fast during the month of Ramadan.
4. Help poor people.
5. If possible, make a *hajj*, or holy journey, to Mecca in Saudi Arabia (see the map).

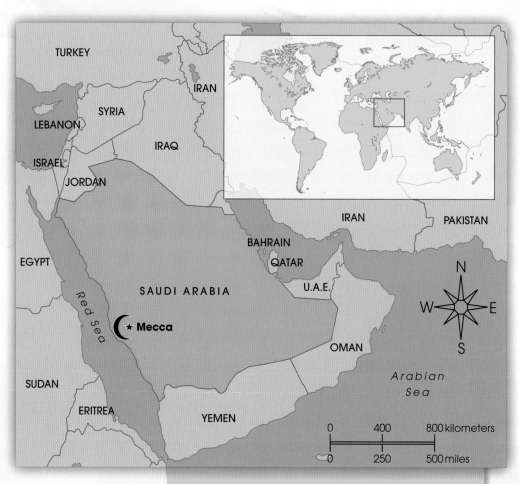

Mecca, Saudi Arabia, is where Muslims travel for their *hajj*.

Mecca is considered Islam's most holy, or sacred, place. Not many Muslims make it to Mecca because it is very expensive to get there. Malcolm's half sister Ella helped pay for Malcolm to travel there. In April 1964 Malcolm made his *hajj* to Mecca.

Life-changing journey to Mecca

Malcolm was amazed by what he found in Mecca. In his journal, Malcolm wrote that Muslims of all colors—from "blue-eyed blonds to black-skinned Africans"—were praying together. There was no separation between blacks and whites. Muslims treated each other like brothers and sisters, no matter what color their skin was. For the first time, Malcolm realized that **integration** of blacks and whites might be possible in the United States.

After his *hajj* Malcolm changed his name to El-Hajj Malik El-Shabazz. "El-Hajj" meant Malcolm had been to Mecca. "Malik" was Arabic for Malcolm. The Shabazz were a tribe of black people who had moved from East Asia to Africa.

After his *hajj*, Malcolm started following the traditional Islam religion. Here Malcolm is wearing a fez, a felt hat worn by men in some Muslim countries.

Martyr

Malcolm returned from his *hajj* with many new ideas. In the **Nation of Islam**, Malcolm had not protested with other groups because Muhammad would not let him. Now he believed more strongly that blacks all over the world needed to unite. In June 1964, Malcolm created the Organization for Afro-American Unity, to fight for black rights worldwide.

Malcolm also realized not all white people are evil. Whites still could not join Malcolm's organizations, but he was willing to work with white **activists** who really wanted **equality** for black people. As he later said, "I can get along with white people who can get along with me."

New supporters, new enemies

As a result of these changes, Malcolm gained new supporters. Some people left the Nation of Islam and joined Muslim Mosque, Inc. Other supporters were middle-class blacks who did not like the **militant** Nation of Islam but now supported Malcolm's new ideas.

Did you know?

Malcolm X had a feeling he would be **assassinated**. He had enemies because of what he believed and how hard he fought for what he believed. In his **autobiography** Malcolm said, "These are ingredients which make it just about impossible for me to die of old age."

Because he spoke for black rights around the world, Malcolm was away from home a lot. Here he spends time with his oldest daughters, Attallah (right) and Quibilah.

Malcolm also gained more enemies. The FBI still thought he was dangerous. With connections worldwide, Malcolm now had more resources to start a **revolution**. Malcolm also had enemies within the Nation of Islam. The **Black Muslims** were not happy that Malcolm was drawing members away. He started receiving death threats on the phone.

Firebomb

Around 3:00 a.m. on February 14, 1965, Malcolm heard an explosion. Someone had thrown a firebomb into his house. Malcolm and his family escaped unharmed, but a large portion of the house was destroyed. Now Malcolm knew for sure that people were trying to kill him.

Assassination

A week later, Malcolm held a meeting at the Audubon Ballroom in Harlem. Malcolm's wife, Betty, took their four daughters to hear him speak. Soon after Malcolm started talking, a man in the front row stood up and started shooting at Malcolm. Then two more men started shooting.

Betty threw herself over the children. Malcolm fell to the stage, but the men kept shooting. Then they ran. The crowd tackled Talmadge Hayer, but the other two men got away and were arrested later. When the shooting stopped, Betty ran up to the stage. It was too late. Malcolm X was dead. He was 39 years old.

Police arrested Talmadge Hayer outside the Audubon Ballroom in 1965. He was released from prison in 2010.

In 1966 Talmadge Hayer, Norman 3X Butler, and Thomas 15X Johnson were sent to jail for killing Malcolm X. Hayer admitted someone paid him to do it, but he would not say who. Butler and Johnson were both members of the Nation of Islam, but they said they were innocent.

Did you know?

If two people named Norman joined the Nation of Islam, the first person was called Norman X. The second person was Norman 2X, and so on.

The Lasting Influence of Malcolm X

Malcolm X was one of the most important leaders of the 20th century. Though Muslim Mosque, Inc., closed after Malcolm died, his message and methods live on.

Black power

Malcolm X was considered the hero of the **black power movement**. This movement started in the 1960s. The main idea behind black power was that black people should be proud of being black. Black people should see themselves as capable of taking charge of their lives.

Members of the black power movement raise a fist as a sign of unity. Some people called it the "black power salute."

Louis Farrakhan

(born 1933)

In the period since Malcolm X's death, Louis Farrakhan has been an important leader among the **Black Muslims**. He was born Louis Walcott in New York. Around 1955 Malcolm X invited Louis to a Black Muslim meeting. Louis soon joined the **Nation of Islam**, and Malcolm became his mentor, or teacher. Later, Louis received the name Louis Farrakhan from Elijah Muhammad.

When Malcolm left the Nation of Islam, Farrakhan criticized Malcolm and warned him there were consequences for being a **traitor**. Malcolm's family believed Farrakhan secretly helped organize Malcolm's death. In 2000 Farrakhan admitted that his words against Malcolm may have led to him being **assassinated**. Farrakhan led the Nation of Islam into the 21st century.

In 1966 the Black Panther Party formed as part of the black power movement. Members of the Black Panthers wore black leather jackets, carried guns, and called themselves "the children of Malcolm." They patrolled the streets of black neighborhoods. They demanded nicer housing for blacks and kept track of police violence against black people. They carried out Malcolm's ideas about fighting for freedom.

Two of Malcolm X's daughters, Ilyasah and Malaak Shabazz, smile at a signing for Ilyasah's book, *Growing Up X*.

Life without Malcolm

Malcolm's wife, Betty, was pregnant at the time Malcolm was assassinated. She gave birth to twin girls in September 1965. Betty raised her six daughters in Mount Vernon, New York. In 1975 she earned a **doctorate** degree in education administration. Then she got a job at Medgar Evers College in Brooklyn in New York City. She worked there for 21 years, first as a professor and then as the director of the department of communications.

Did you know?

Betty fought to get a high school named after her husband. There is now a Malcolm X Shabazz High School in Newark, New Jersey.

Betty shares Malcolm's message

Betty spent time spreading her husband's inspirational message to black people. She spoke at high school and college graduation ceremonies. She hosted a radio show for black women. She wanted people to remember what Malcolm taught about black people taking charge of their lives.

Betty also worked with Coretta Scott King and Myrlie Evers-Williams. Coretta was the wife of Martin Luther King, Jr., who was assassinated in 1968. Myrlie was the wife of Medgar Evers, a civil rights leader who was assassinated in 1963. These three women spent more than 30 years working for black rights.

Betty died in 1997, but Malcolm's message lives on through books and films. Malcolm's **autobiography** was published shortly after his death and became a national bestseller.

After Malcolm's death, Betty and her six daughters all took the last name Shabazz. This was the name Malcolm starting using after his *hajj*.

Timeline

1916
Marcus Garvey comes to the United States and starts teaching about black nationalism.

1925
Malcolm Little (later Malcolm X) is born.

1931
Malcolm's father is found dead on streetcar tracks.

1939
Malcolm's mother is sent to a mental institution. Malcolm goes to a group home in Mason, Michigan.

1941
Malcolm quits school and moves to Boston.

1953
Elijah Muhammad makes Malcolm assistant minister of Detroit Temple Number One.

1952
Malcolm meets Elijah Muhammad and changes his name to Malcolm X.

1952
August
Malcolm is released from jail. He moves to Detroit, Michigan.

1948-1949
Malcolm converts to the Nation of Islam while in prison.

1946
Malcolm is sentenced to 10 years in jail.

1954
May
The *Brown v. Board of Education* lawsuit rules segregation of schools is unconstitutional.

1954
June
Malcolm becomes minister of Harlem Temple Number Seven.

1955
Rosa Parks refuses to give up her seat on a Montgomery, Alabama, bus. Many people view this as the start of the civil rights movement.

1957
Malcolm stands up to the police in Harlem.

1963
Martin Luther King, Jr., leads the March on Washington.

1960
The FBI starts spying on Malcolm.

1959
The documentary *The Hate That Hate Produced* appears on television.

1958
Malcolm marries Betty Sanders.

1957
Elijah Muhammad makes Malcolm the national representative for the Nation of Islam.

1963
September 15
Four black girls are killed when the Sixteenth Street Baptist Church in Birmingham, Alabama, is bombed.

1963
November 22
President Kennedy is assassinated.

1964
February
Cassius Clay defeats Sonny Liston, then announces his new name is Muhammad Ali.

1964
March
Malcolm leaves the Nation of Islam and forms Muslim Mosque, Inc.

1965
February 21
Malcolm X is assassinated at the Audubon Ballroom in Harlem.

1965
February 14
Malcolm's house is firebombed.

1964
July
The Civil Rights Act makes discrimination based on race illegal.

1964
June
Malcolm forms the Organization for Afro-American Unity.

1964
April
Malcolm makes his *hajj* to Mecca.

Family Tree

Earl Little (1890–1931) = Louise Norton Little (1900–1991)

Shelman Sandlin (1913–1986) = Ollie Mae Sanders

Malcolm X (1925–1965) = Betty Sanders X (1936–1997)

Attallah Shabazz (born 1958)

Quibilah Shabazz (born 1960)

Ilyasah Shabazz (born 1962)

Gamilah Shabazz (born 1964)

Malaak Shabazz (born 1965)

Malikah Shabazz (born 1965)

Malcolm Shabazz (born 1984)

Glossary

activist person who speaks or acts to help a group of people or some other cause

assassinate to kill, often for political reasons

autobiography book that someone writes about his or her own life

Black Muslim member of the Nation of Islam

black nationalism belief that black people should live separately from white people, with their own black leaders, schools, and businesses

black power movement movement in the 1960s that grew out of the civil rights movement; it spread ideas of black pride and independence, and its symbol was a raised black fist

civil rights movement organized protest movement of the 1950s and 1960s with the goal to end segregation and discrimination against black people

convert to change from one religion or set of beliefs to another

discrimination negative treatment of a person or group of people based on a characteristic such as race or religion

doctorate highest academic degree someone can earn

documentary factual film that is based on research and written or recorded documents

equality being the same or equal in terms of rank, opportunities or rights

hajj holy journey to Mecca that is one of the five duties of every Muslim

integration mixing together of races in neighborhoods, schools, and so on

Islam religion based on the belief that Allah is God and Muhammad is his prophet; followers are called Muslims

Jim Crow laws laws created to keep the races separate and discriminate against black people

lynch to kill someone for something he or she supposedly did; lynching is usually performed by a mob, or group, without legal authority

militant aggressive; ready to fight

Muslim person who follows the religion of Islam

Nation of Islam religion based on the belief that blacks are Allah's chosen people, and they should separate themselves from white people; followers are called Black Muslims

race group of people who share similar characteristics such as skin color and whose distant relatives come from the same geographical area

revolution sudden or complete change in the leadership of a city, state, or nation; revolution usually happens through fighting

segregation forced separation of races

sit-in type of nonviolent protest in which people sit in a business or street until they are forced to leave

slave person who has his or her life, liberty, and fortune controlled by another person

slavery relationship in which one person has absolute power over another and controls his or her life, liberty, and fortune

traitor someone who betrays another person or group of people

welfare food or other necessities the state provides to poor people

white supremacist person who thinks white people are better than nonwhite people

zoot suit man's suit in which the jacket has thick shoulder pads and the pants are very narrow at the ankles

Find Out More

Books

Gormley, Beatrice. *Malcolm X: A Revolutionary Voice*. New York: Sterling Publishing, 2008.

Gunderson, Jessica. *X: A Biography of Malcolm X*. Mankato, Minn., Capstone Press, 2011.

Meany, John. *Has the Civil Rights Movement Been Successful?* Chicago, Heinemann, 2009.

Price, Sean Stewart. *When Will I Get In? Segregation and Civil Rights*. Chicago: Raintree, 2007.

DVDs

Malcolm X. Warner Bros., 1992.
(NOTE: This film has some mature content. Talk to a parent or guardian about watching this film.)

Websites

Malcolm X Official Website
www.malcolmx.com/index.html
This is the official website of Malcolm X. Click on the links to find out more about Malcolm's background, famous quotes, photographs, a timeline, and more.

Malcolm X Biography
www.biography.com/articles/Malcolm-X-9396195
This website provides a short video on Malcolm's life, as well as a written biography.

African American World for Kids
http://pbskids.org/aaworld/index.html
Visit this website to learn more about important events in African American history.

School Desegregation
http://pbskids.org/wayback/civilrights/features_school.html
Learn about nine brave students who stood up against school segregation during the civil rights movement in 1957.

Places to visit

Malcolm X House Site
3448 Pinkney Street
Omaha, NE 68111
www.nps.gov/nr/travel/civilrights/ne1.htm

Martin Luther King Jr. National Historic Site
450 Auburn Avenue, NE
Atlanta, GA 30312
404-331-5190
www.nps.gov/nr/travel/civilrights/g1.htm

Sixteenth Street Baptist Church
Corner of 16th Street and 6th Avenue
Birmingham, AL 35203
205-251-9402
www.nps.gov/nr/travel/civilrights/al11.htm

National Civil Rights Museum
450 Mulberry
Memphis, TN 38103
901-521-9699
www.civilrightsmuseum.org/

Index